SAMUEL O. OLULANA

You Are BORN TO BE GREAT

YOU ARE BORN TO BE GREAT

Copyright **[c]** 2014 by:
SAMUEL O. OLULANA
ISBN: 978-978-51395-1-8

NEW AND IMPROVED EDITION:
     April 2017

Published in Nigeria by:
Treasured Word Publishing House

All Rights Reserved
Before any portion of this book can be used, written permission must be secured from the author or publisher, except for brief excerpt in magazine, articles, reviews etc.

All Scripture quotations, unless otherwise indicated are from the NEW KING JAMES VERSION of the Bible.

For Enquiries Write:
Treasured Word Publishing House
P. O . BOX 7035 Sapon,
Abeokuta, Ogun State
Nigeria.

Tel: 0813 666 2194; 0813 665 9832
E-mail: twph2013@gmail.com
Website: www.treasuredword.net

This Book Is A
GIFT

To

From

On The Occasion Of

Date

When Others Are Saying There Is A Casting down, You Shall Say There Is A Lifting Up

You Are Born To Be Great

Introduction 7

<u>YOU ARE BORN TO BE GREAT - Chapter One</u>
God Has A Purpose For Creating You 17

<u>YOU ARE BORN TO BE GREAT - Chapter Two</u>
Why Many People Fail In The Race Of Life 53

<u>YOU ARE BORN TO BE GREAT - Chapter Three</u>
Steps To Greatness 83

<u>YOU ARE BORN TO BE GREAT - Chapter Four</u>
The In-evitable 113

You Are Born To Be Great

Introduction

Everyone that is born of God is destined to become great in life. God is a great God, and it is only natural to expect Him to give birth to great individuals because, like always beget like. So, for the great God to give birth to failures will amount to a great disgrace. The great God can never give birth to failures.

For instance; the child of a goat must look and behave like a goat. Also, the

You Are Born To Be Great

child of a monkey must look and behave like a monkey. If the child of a goat looks and behave like a monkey then, something must be wrong somewhere. As a child of God, it is only natural that you should look, behave, and become a success like God, your Father. Anything that is different to this makes you a bastard. No wonder God created each one of us in His image.

So God created man in his own image, in the image of God created he him; male an female created he them.
Gen. 1:27

There is no one born of God who is programmed to become a second best. No, every child of God is born to occupy a place of royalty. You are born to show

Introduction

forth the glory of God in this dying world. Anything contrary to this, is a gift from the devil. No amount of excuse or explanation will make it become right at any time, and at any place. The word of God says:

But ye are a chosen generation, a royal priesthood, an holy nation, a peculiar people; that <u>ye should shew forth the praises of him who hath called you out of darkness into his marvelous light</u>:
1 Peter 2:9

The truth you need to believe is that God has a very unique plan for each of His children. There is nowhere in the world where exists another you. You are very unique and special to God. Someone else may look like you but he cannot be you.

You Are Born To Be Great

You are very unique and special. In the original plan of God, He has a special plan for a special you, which is not meant for any other person but you.

In the book of Jeremiah chapter twenty nine, and in verse eleven, the living word of the only living and true God says:

For I know the thoughts I think towards you, saith the Lord, <u>thoughts of peace and not of evil,</u> to give you an expected end.

Jer. 29:11

Friend, God has a special plan for you. It is not an evil plan. It is the best of plan you can ever imagine. God's plan is to make you great. He wants you to become the reference point of every good thing you can ever think of.

Introduction

Hear this: right from the very beginning of your existence, God has in His wisdom, determined what your end will be. He has programmed you for success. And it is an enviable success. There is no devil that has the power to change or alter it without your active approval.

The implication of this is that, since His original plan for you is to become great, that means you have no choice other than to become great in life. You must aspire to become what God has made you no matter what happens to you in the journey of life. You must learn how to turn every obstacle that showed up on your way to greatness into a very good stepping stone into your God-ordained, very glorious future.

You Are Born To Be Great

Every wise manufacturer for instance, determines the purpose of his products before manufacturing it. In the same way, God has determined your purpose before you were born. You cannot change it no matter what you do. So, it is sure that no devil can change it either.

God is the wisest manufacturer you can ever imagine. He is such a wise God that everything He manufactured is very good. There is nowhere His work has been faulted for once. This shows that you are not just created for the fun of creation, you are created on purpose; you are well formed to perform a great assignment in the end-time agenda of the Almighty God.

It does not matter the problem you are

Introduction

faced with presently; your present financial situation, no matter how bad it may look like, is not an indication that God does not have a good plan for you.

Your present challenge, no matter how bad it may look to your human judgement and reasoning, is nothing but the necessary and the needed platform that is needed for you to be able to enter into your God ordained, very glorious, and very wonderful success plan.

Devil knows this and that is why he is doing all he could to make you think that you have a special problem. No, my friend, you don't have a special problem. Whatever you are going through now is just a common challenge. 1 Cor. 10:13

As you go through the pages of this Life-

You Are Born To Be Great

Transforming book, my heart felt prayer is that you will discover His purpose for your life and walk in it by divine guidance to His glory and for your goodness in Jesus name.

You will surely succeed because that is why God has created you. I curse every form of opposition to your success in Jesus name.

You are welcome to the "City of Success" in Jesus name.

You Are Born To Be Great

Chapter 1
God Created You For A Purpose

We have been able to establish very convincingly, right from the introduction of this life-transforming book that God created you for a glorious purpose, and that two of you has never existed at any point. Anyone may look like you anywhere, but the truth is that he or she is not the **REAL** you. You are the only one of your kind on this planet earth. Wonderful!

In this chapter, by the help of the Holy

You Are Born To Be Great

Spirit, I want to show you that you are not created for the fun of creation, but, you are actually created by God to be great, and that you have no other choice than to become great in life. That seed of greatness in you will not die in Jesus name.

Consider this: all the host in the kingdom of the devil put together with the devil himself leading them, are too small to stop the ability of the Almighty God that is inside of you. This is one revelation that has the capacity to launch you into your great future if you can assimilate it.

Friend, you are not an ordinary creature because, you carry something that is very great inside of you which is crying

God Created You For A Purpose

for expression. It is called the power of God. It is God's anointing for greatness. It is deposited in you by God so that you can fly high in life. If there is only one person that will succeed in your generation, then, that one person is you. This is because you already carry the seed of success.

Whatever the Lord has done, the bible has made us to understand that they are permanent. This means that since God has made you to be great in life, that is the only thing that must happen to you. Anything that is contrary to what God has made you is not from God and you must do your best to reject it. No man will do that for you. It is a responsibility that is meant for you to perform. You must be ready to dare the lies of the

You Are Born To Be Great

devil and get them back to the owner - the devil.

Friend, it is your responsibility to say no to everything that is contrary to the plan of God for you. God has given you all the needed weapons you will ever need to counter and conquer every devices of your enemy. If you fail to use them, then, you will pay dearly for your negligence.

The truth is this: what you don't want, you must not watch. The situation you don't like, and you refuse to challenge, has every right to remain with you. And every challenge from the enemy you fail to confront you cannot conquer. Please, refuse to accept any form of defeat because you are not made to be pitied; you are rather made to be envied. The

God Created You For A Purpose

generation that is coming afer you must hear about you.

According to the word of God, which is found in the book of Jeremiah, it is written:

For I know the thoughts I think towards you, saith the Lord, thoughts of peace and not of evil, to give you an expected end.
Jer. 29:11

Friend, your future is very important to God and that is why He has taken His time to work it out for you gloriously. God has designed the future of each one of us very specially. And it is to show forth His glory through us in this dying world.

You Are Born To Be Great

Friend, you are created to enjoy the best of God in this dark world. You have been made to be the light and the salt of the world. This simply means that the world is to look unto you in every area of your endeavour. You cannot afford to fail in this great assignment. You are the head. You must not allow any situation to dispossess you of your birthright opportunities.

However, for you to enter into the glorious future God has planned for you, and enjoy it to the maximum, you have to undertake the task of discovering it. Yes, it is true that a glorious future has already been created for you, but you have to discover it. Otherwise you may be living another man's life.

God Created You For A Purpose

Please, know that your redemption is not for fun. God has not redeemed you at such a high cost because He was jobless or because He does not know where to invest His energy and resources. He has rather redeemed you so that you may become what He has designed you to become in life. Everything about you has been made perfectly well at redemption. Redemption actually reposition you for the exploits God has created you for.

Friend, do you know that when the purpose of a thing is not known the abuse of its use is inevitable? In the same way, if you don't know why you are redeemed, you may not live to actualize the reason why God redeemed you. I pray that the investments of God over

You Are Born To Be Great

you will not result into a waste in Jesus name.

The following are among the reasons why God has paid so much to redeem you. Your understanding of each one of them has the potential to fire you up very dangerously to the extent that you will become an untouchable element to the devil and failure.

YOU ARE REDEEMED TO SUCCEED.

God has made you to succeed in life and anything short of success is not from Him; it must have come from the devil. It is your duty or responsibility to reject it because it does not belong to you. Every gift that is not good never comes from God. He is a good God, and it is only natural to expect good things from Him.

God Created You For A Purpose

It is a well known fact that a good tree will never produce a bad fruit.

This is the way the word of Life puts it:

Every good gift and every perfect gift is from above, and it cometh down from the Father of lights, with whom is no variableness, neither shadow of turning.
James 1:17 [KJV]

The word of God clearly showed us that God wants everyone of His dear children to succeed and that is the absolute truth.

The Bible in the book of third John says:

Beloved, I wish above all things that thou mayest prosper and be in health, even as thy soul prospereth.
3 John 2

You Are Born To Be Great

The mind of God is made known to us through His living word. It is now your responsibility to make sure that you walk according to what His word says. If you fail to do this, you have succeeded in allowing the devil to rob you of God's glory for your life. And it will interest you to know that God cannot come down and help you do it. You must refuse to smell the food you are not prepare to eat.

Please understand that in the kingdom of God, everything that happens is always guided by Divine principles. And there is nothing you can do to change any of them. There are things you must do, and there are things that God will do. If you leave what you are expected to do undone there is nothing God can do to help you about that.

God Created You For A Purpose

For instance, no matter how much you love your wife or husband, you cannot go to the toilet on his or her behalf. In the same way, even though God loves you so much, He cannot on your behalf do what He has commanded you to do. You must be ready to take responsibilities for every issues of your life. You cannot afford to fail in this great assignment.
Right where you are now, if there is a mirror very close to you, lift up your eyes and look at the man you see in the mirror and say to him that he will succeed if he can be bold to be responsible.

If there is no mirror close to you, place your right hand upon your head and declare to that head that he will definitely become great if he dare to become responsible.

You Are Born To Be Great

YOU ARE REDEEMED TO SHOW FORTH GOD'S GLORY IN THIS DARK WORLD.

Through the following scriptures you will discover that the plan of God for your life is very glorious. You are a candidate for God's glory. And as long as you can play your part as He commands you, nothing will be able to stop you from succeeding in this world. This is the absolute truth.

The word of God says:

Having predestinated us unto the adoption of children by Jesus Christ to himself, according to the good pleasure of his will

To the <u>praise</u> of the glory of his grace,

God Created You For A Purpose

wherein he hath made us accepted in the beloved.
Eph. 1:5-6

The word of God also says:

In whom also we have obtained an inheritance, being predestinated according to the purpose of him who worketh all things after the counsel of his own will.

That we should be to <u>the praise</u> of his glory, who first trusted in Christ.
Eph. 1:11-12

Yet at another place in the Scriptures, the word of God also says:

As ye know how we exhorted and comfort and charged every one of you, as a father doth his children.

You Are Born To Be Great

That ye would walk worthy of God, who hath called you unto his kingdom and glory.
1 Thess. 2:11-12

Friend, ever before the foundation of the earth, everything concerning you was perfected. However, you must be ready to take responsibility for the issues of your life. God has done His part, you cannot afford to waste all His efforts over you. You must rise up like the son of the mighty God today, so that you may recover your destiny from the destructive plan of the enemy because, nothing kills a man like complacency.

YOU ARE REDEEMED TO BE A GOOD EXAMPLE IN EVERYTHING YOU DO.

God Created You For A Purpose

You are redeemed to be a good example to your world in every area of your endeavours. God has designed you to show your world the best way to live and do things. You are the one your world should copy in everything. You have been equipped with everything that you need to succeed in life. This is one truth the devil will never allow you to accept and yet, it is the real truth that you need to put him [the devil] where he truly belongs.

Let no man despise thy youth; but <u>be thou an example</u> of the believers, in word, in conversation, in charity, in spirit, in faith, in purity.
1 Tim. 4:12

God has not redeemed you to fail, rather,

You Are Born To Be Great

you have been born to rule and dominate in life. If you can take a good care of the above instructions of God, you will surely excel in life. You are to be an example to your world in the way you speak, discuss, in love, in the things of the Spirit, in faith, and in purity. You have to stop playing the role of a second best from now.

Please, know that no man has ever been disappointed by the thoughts of his mind. If you think you are a nobody that is exactly what you will become but, if you think you are someone to be reckoned with, that is what you will become. No wonder the bible says that a man is always a product of his thoughts.

Failure of any type is not in the original

God Created You For A Purpose

plan of God for any of His children. You are the light of the world. You are made to show-case the glory of God in this decayed and dying world. Every genuine born again child of God is a special person. He is an heaven made champion. And as we all know, whatever is from above is above all.

You are a product made from the higher wisdom; there is no single fault in your make-up. You are what you are called by God irrespective of what anybody says. The Bible says:

For thou art an holy people unto the lord thy God and the lord hath chosen thee to be a peculiar people unto himself, above all the nation that are upon the earth.
Deut. 14:2

You Are Born To Be Great

God's word also says:

But ye are a chosen generation, a royal priesthood an holy nation, a peculiar people; that ye should shew forth the praises of him who hath called you out of darkness into his marvelous light.
1 Peter 2:9

Consider the following statements very well because they have the potential to give you a glorious future. Please, play no joke with anyone of them because they are Holy Spirit inspired. They are meant to give you the needed speed to take over from your enemy and bring joy to your maker.

1. The plan of God for you as one of His dear children is that you, as His ambassador in this world, should become great in life just as your Father is

God Created You For A Purpose

great. This is the absolute truth. Please, take your time and meditate over this. No wonder God commanded you and I to have dominion over the earth because, He has put inside us the seed of greatness.

2. The plan of God for you is the best of plan which can ever happen to you under heaven. Anything contrary to the plan of God for you is a fake. You must make up your mind to be the best which God has prepared for you. No fake product will ever be able to perform like the original. Be very careful about this. Be yourself and give out the best in you.

3. The plan of God for you is the cheapest way to move you forward to the topmost top. Any other plan is a fake, and any

You Are Born To Be Great

other way you take will give you a lot of stress and struggles, with many disappointments. It may even kill you.

4. The plan of God for you is God's blue print to give you a glorious life. There is no other plan you can invent for yourself or any man can give to you that can ever be equal to the good plan which God has already made available to you. So, try and see that you guide it jealously.

Consider the following word of God also.

It says:

And God bless them and God said unto them, be fruitful and multiply and replenish the earth and subdue it: and have dominion over the fish of the sea and over the fowl of the air and over

God Created You For A Purpose

every living thing that moveth upon the earth.

Gen. 1:28

After creating man, the bible showed us that the next thing God did was to bless man,(either by praying or by giving gifts to them, I don't know). Thereafter, God gave man **FIVE** major assignments or responsibilities to perform before man can live in dominion. The truth therefore, is that any man or woman, young or old, who is able to perform to detail, these five major responsibilities successfully, will without doubt become great in life. The devil and all the activities of his evil angels notwithstanding.

THE FIVE RESPONSIBILITIES.

You Are Born To Be Great

God has given unto His children commandments for different areas of our life. But I want to share with you FIVE major commandments God gave us as it relates to our subject of discussion, which we must fulfill before any man can live in Dominion or in greatness. They are the following:

1. GO AND BE FRUITFUL.

The first commandment of God to man after creation was to go and be fruitful. To be fruitful is to have result in whatever you do. It is not all about bearing children. When there is no fruit in what you are then, men will say you are a failure.

It is the commandment of God for all His

God Created You For A Purpose

children to be fruitful and you have no reason to live as a failure. If you do, you have turn God into a liar. We all know that God cannot lie, so, something must be wrong somewhere if you fail and if you trace it well, you will find out that it will have it's source in you.

Do you know why? It is because, God has invested in you everything that you will ever need to become great. It is youR duty to locate your God-given potentials and use them for your fruitfulness.

2. GO AND MULTIPLY

As a child of God, He has also commanded you to "go and multiply". Multiplication as we know is talking about visible increase. Stagnation of any type therefore, is not your portion.

You Are Born To Be Great

Retrogression is not the plan of God for any of His children. The only thing that is expected from you as a child of God is all-round increase.

It does not matter the situation you are facing presently, the truth is that you will make it to the top whether the devil like it or not in Jesus name. What you must know is that the devil is too small to stop the power of God inside of you from performing the intention of God concerning you. Therefore, as you put that power of God - the gift of God - in you to work from now, you will experience Divinely multiplication in Jesus name.

3. GO AND REPLENISH THE EARTH

You are also commanded by God to replenish the earth. You are to make the

God Created You For A Purpose

earth a good place to live in for all and sundry.

To replenish simply means to make something full again by replacing everything that has been used up. You are therefore commanded to be among the other children of God that will make sure that the entire world is inhabited to the glory of God. There are areas which are meant for you to rule over.

Setting the pace therefore for others to follow, is one of your assignments here on earth. You will not fail in Jesus name.

4. GO AND 'FIGHT' YOUR WAY THROUGH (SUBDUE YOUR OPPOSITIONS)

Perhaps, the most challenging of the responsibilities God gave to man is that

You Are Born To Be Great

man should rise up and subdue all the forces that want to stop him from going forward in life. I want you to know that God will never have given man this great assignment except for the fact that He knew that man has been equipped for it.

This goes to show us that for you to be able to subdue any force that rises against you in the course of your assignment or job, you must be ready to fight.

Please, know that even though God has given you a promise that is not a proof that you will have it. You can only possess what God has given to you if you are ready to stand up and take responsibility of contending with every negative forces that may come across

God Created You For A Purpose

your way.

The word of God says:

Rise ye up, take your journey, and pass over the river Arnon: behold, I have given into thine hand Sihon the Amorite, king of Heshbon, and his land: begin to possess it, <u>and contend with him in battle.</u>
Deut. 2:24

From the above word of God, we can see that before the people could take possession of the land God has given to them, they must be ready to fight against their enemies who were occupying the land. If they fail to undertake this great responsibility they will never be able to take possession of the land God has given them.

You Are Born To Be Great

This is to show you that you cannot really enjoy all that the Lord has given to you except you are ready to fight against all oppositions as they show up on your way. This is very important. Your duty or responsibility is to rely on the ability of God in you all the time, and confront any situation that want to stop your success. You will not fail in Jesus name.

5. GO AND DOMINATE (ESTABLISH YOUR PROMINENCE)

To dominate simply means to live in a position whereby you are actually in charge of the affairs of your life. You determine what must happen around you and not the other way round. Situations and circumstances around you must bow to your decision, and not

God Created You For A Purpose

you crying under their demands.

This position of dominion is not available to a lazy and foolish Christian. It is only available to the very diligent, faithful, obedient, and righteous child of God.

You cannot live in dominion if your ways are crooked or perverted. You must be an obedient child of God and you must walk in love and complete obedience to His word. May God grant you knowledge and understanding concerning what we are sharing here in Jesus name.

Friend, please take note of this very important point: the reason why many are not living in dominion today is simply because they have not been able to subdue their challenges. And until

You Are Born To Be Great

they subdue those challenges which life has brought their way, they will remain subdued by those challenges.

Please, know also that you cannot wear any crown of victory until you have fought your way through every obstacles that comes across your way. Let me show you right now how you can fight your way through every obstacles that comes across your way in the journey of life. I can tell you confidently that no force has the power to stop you from going forward if you can take your stand with God. I pray that God will help you in Jesus name.

HOW DO I FIGHT MY WAY THROUGH?

If you live in Nigeria for instance, you will agree with me that the way you

God Created You For A Purpose

prepare rice is not the same way you prepare beans. There are different procedures to follow when you want to prepare any one of them. There is nothing you can do to change this no matter who you are.

In the same way, for you to subdue your challenges, God has laid down strategies for you to use as occasion demands. Any other strategies you invent by yourself or any man invent for you will give you nothing but a great disappointment. I want you to take your time and ponder over this simple fact very well.

The word of God says:

Then he answered and spake unto me, saying, this is the word of the lord unto Zerubbabel, saying, Not by

You Are Born To Be Great

might, nor by power, but by my spirit, saith the lord of hosts.

Zech. 4:6

The word of God says that your might and strength will fail you if you rely on them. Your certificate is too small to give you the dimension of greatness God has in stock for you.

The greatness I am talking about here is not a function of your monthly salary. No matter how much you may be earning per month, you cannot achieve the level of greatness I am talking about here.

God is the giver of the greatness I am talking about here. For you to get your portion, you must be ready to align yourself with the instructions of God. You must do what He commands before

God Created You For A Purpose

you can become what He has made you.

The following word of God gives us a vivid answer to the point I am trying to show you. It says:

And I will give unto thee the keys of the kingdom of heaven: and whatsoever thou shalt bound on earth shall be bound in heaven: and whatsoever thou shalt loose on earth shall be loosed in heaven.
Matth. 16:19

There are different Divine keys to open different doors of blessings. There are many keys for you to use in order to secure your victory and greatness in the areas of your desires here on earth.

What is the purpose of these keys? The

You Are Born To Be Great

purpose of these keys is to give you dominion in the areas of your desired blessings. There are many keys for you to use in order to secure your victory and greatness. So, the devil is a known looser as far as your success and greatness in life is concerned. The purpose of these keys also, is to give you dominion in the areas of life that you have challenges and establish your dominion.

For instance, the key that will give you financial abundance is different from the key that will give you a sickness free life. There are different Divine keys for different doors of blessing. The one you have is the one you can use. One thing that I want you to know at this point is that you are only limited by the extent of the knowledge you have about every

God Created You For A Purpose

given area of your needs and challenges. When you know enough, you will dominate without any stress.

Hear me; no devil is your problem. Your real problem is ignorance. And the only way to cure it is by acquiring more knowledge in the areas you are having challenges. No amount of prayer will impart knowledge into your brain. You have to sit down and consciously acquire it through reading and meditation.

You Are Born To Be Great

Why Many People Are Not Successful In Life

By the grace of God, I will be sharing with you at least SIX reasons why many people fail in life in this chapter. And I sincerely hope they will be a very good guide to you if you don't want to fail also.

Please, understand right from here that ***success is a choice and failure is also a choice.*** The most stricken thing is that you will always get your choice materialized in

You Are Born To Be Great

your life no matter what happened. It may take some time to show up, but the truth is that it will surely show up.

Friend, I want you to know that if there is no fire burning somewhere, then it will be very difficult for you to notice any smoke anywhere. This is a hard truth, but it is the truth that cannot be denied by anybody at any time. You will always become what you chose to become in life.

Let us now examine these reasons one before the other. My prayer is that God will help you to gain a good understanding from each one of them in Jesus name. Because, I believe this will help you to guide against the occurrence of any of these mistakes.

Why Many People Are Not Successful In Life

1. WALKING CONTRARY TO THE WILL OF GOD

There are many people who have failed very woefully in life not because they are lazy, or because they don't know what they should do, or because they are from any of the third world countries, but simply because they have missed the plan of God for their lives.

There are two categories of people in this group. The first group are the ones who have failed to discover God's plan for their lives but are just walking according to what they could see or imagined is good. The second group are the ones who knows the will of God and refused to walk in. Either of the two groups above will earn you a straight ticket to the city of frustration

You Are Born To Be Great

because it is one thing for you to know what you should do, it is yet another thing for you to do it. I want you to know that walking contrary to the will of God for your life is the fastest route to the land of failure.

Also, many other people have succeeded beyond human imagination, not because they are too good, or because they are genius, or because they are from the so-called advanced countries of the world, but simply because they are walking in line with the plan of God for their lives. The amazing truth is that when any bird decided to flow in the direction of the wind, that bird will surely have a smooth as well as a trouble-free ride. This is simply showing you that as long as you are walking in the will of God for your life you

Why Many People Are Not Successful In Life

will enjoy the support as well as the sponsorship of God.

Friend, you may not like what I am about to tell you now, but whether you like it or not is not important because it is the truth. Until you fall in line with the will of God for your life, you may be chasing the shadow of greatness and breakthrough for eternity to come.

The above statement may sound very hard, but it is the plain as well as the hard truth. Whether you as a person like it or not is a secondary consideration. Whether you like it or not the truth will always prevail anywhere because you cannot change the truth know matter how hard you try. Every wise people knows that it is in their best interest to always align with the truth.

You Are Born To Be Great

When you attempt to walk against the truth, you will surely suffer many losses.

CONSIDER THIS TESTIMONY

I was in a meeting at Gateway hotel Abeokuta sometimes ago, and a young man came up to the platform to testify to the goodness of God in his life. It was a testimony that I strongly believe will help you to understand what I am saying here more clearly and convincingly, because there is nothing that reveals the truth more than true life experiences.

This boy according to his testimony graduated as a medical doctor, but things were not just working for him the way he desired it; so he decided to seek the face of God for a way out. He declared a three days fasting and prayer for himself.

He said he was shocked beyond measure when the Lord told him on the third day of his fasting and praying that He has never created him as a medical doctor but as an artist. What a wonderful and amazing life-changing revelation.

You may be in this brother's position as you are reading this book, but what you must realize is that all hope is not lost for you. If you can take the steps this brother took you will enjoy the change he experienced. God is still a good God till tomorrow.

This brother went on further to say that God told him that He allowed him to fulfil his personal desire, [like many other people] which can never earn him God

You Are Born To Be Great

greatness. This simply means that his greatness is not tied to medical practice but by walking in the will of God. God now told him to start practicing as an artist which he did.

The good news about the whole thing according to his testimony is that within the first three months of doing what God has designed him for, he bought his first car; a Mercedes 230 car, from the profit he made from designing and selling T-Shirts. Wonderful!

Hear this from me beloved; it is never too late for you to do what is right because, no matter how much you try, what is not right will remain wrong until a correction is made to put it right. And no matter how deep your wrong is, there is still room for you to effect a change. It will never be too late for you to correct a wrong as long as you are still living.

Listen to me: whatever is your qualification as you are reading through this book, my sincere advise to you as a child of God is that you should create the time to know whether you are in God's will or not. Otherwise, you may be embarking on a journey that has no clear destination. You may end up chasing the shadow of greatness until Jesus comes or until death comes to take you home.

2. WRONG ASSOCIATION

A wise man has said: 'show me your friend and I will show you who you are'. This may sound funny, but it is the absolute truth. The association you keep at any point can

You Are Born To Be Great

make or mar your glorious destiny. It is therefore very important for you to see to it that you take your care and determine consciously the type of friends you will keep.

You see, the friendship you keep will go a long way to determine even to a very large extent what your future will look like. Wrong association is one of the reasons why many people have ended their life as gallant losers.

I want to let you know that if you decide to keep company with friends that have no plan for their future, no matter how beautiful your future plan may look, it will be corrupted ultimately. The truth is that many of the people who have failed woefully in life did not fail because they

Why Many People Are Not Successful In Life

don't know what to do, but because they chose to walk with the wrong people. Wrong association always put upon a man the garment of a failure.

Also, many other people who have succeeded in life did not succeed because they are very good, or because they came from a very good back-ground but simply because they chose to keep company with the right people.

Friend, it will not be an exaggeration to say that the association you keep will either make you become great or destroy completely your God ordained glorious future. This may sound too hard, but it is the hard truth which is meant to shape your life for a glorious future.

You Are Born To Be Great

The bible says:

And Lot also, which went with Abram, had flocks, and herds, and tents.

And the land was not able to bear them, that they might dwell together: for their substance was great, so that they could not dwell together.
Gen. 13:5-6

Friend, if your desire is to succeed in life, then, you must be very careful with the association you will keep from now. Don't waste your glorious future carousing in the midst of men and women of shady characters because it has nothing to give you other than failure at the end..

The word of God says:

Why Many People Are Not Successful In Life

He that walk with the wise will be wise but the companion of fools shall be destroyed.
Proverb 13:20

Hear this: friendship is expected to be by a conscious as well as a personal choice, it must not be a function of any force or intimidation. There must not be anything emotional about it. It must be purely based on merit. You must be convinced that the association you are into is going to be for your good.

Hear this from me and hear it very well; any association you keep that is not adding something good to your life, should be done away with right now without a second thought because you don't need it. No matter the people in that group, once you

You Are Born To Be Great

are not deriving any good thing from it you must get out of that group for your own good.

I once had a friend who use to say that if any of his friends is rich and he is not benefitting from it, if that riches is gone into the thin air it is not bad. You may be wondering why he speaks like that. What he is trying to say is that what is the reason of walking with a rich man when his riches cannot benefit you. In other words, he is not ready to keep a company that does not have any benefit to add to his life. In the same way, if you notice that your walking with a particular friend of yours cannot have any good impact on you, the best you can do to help yourself is to quit that relationship immediately.

Why Many People Are Not Successful In Life

May be I should remind you of something important here: You have only one life to live. Please, do your best to live it on purpose. Make sure you touch the lives of people positively. Don't allow foolishness to turn you into an object of shame or pity. Make God to be proud of you.

3. THE FEAR OF WHAT MAN MAY DO

Another reason is the fear of what men may do above what God can do. Many people have failed in life because they fear the men they can see above the Almighty God they cannot see with their two eyes open.

Can you believe that there are many times God will give some people very clear instructions as to what He wants them to do, but they will not do them because they don't want to offend the people around them. Such people don't want people around them to feel bad even when they know that those people cannot help them when the consequence of their disobedience comes upon them. What a foolish way to live and waste a glorious destiny.

For instance, King Saul failed woefully and very wonderfully too, simply because he chose to fear men above God. King Saul decided to go with the opinion of men at the expense of the instruction of God to him. Amazingly, when God rejected Saul as a king over His people, none of his friends, kinsmen, and allies, who collaborated with him to disobey God could help him out. They all watched him fizzle out from glory to a nobody. I believe you don't want your life to end like that of Saul. My prayer for you is that God will give you the grace to get it right.

The word of God says:

> ***And Saul said unto Samuel, I have sinned: for I have transgressed the commandment of the lord, and thy words: because I feared the people, and obeyed their voice.***
> ***1 Samuel 15:24***

Do you know the amazing thing that happened to King Saul? When God rejected him as king over His people, none of the people he didn't want to offend in the first place could help him out. In fact, no one out of all of them was bothered about what

You Are Born To Be Great

happened to him. Some of them will even laugh at him. They all watched him fizzle out into total destruction. That will not be your portion in Jesus name.

Friend, please understand that if you fail people will talk about you, and if you succeed they will talk about you also. I think the best thing is for you to succeed and allow them to talk about your success rather than allow them talk about your failure.

King Saul started with God, but ended his life by talking to the witch. This is a great tragedy. If you don't want to experience the same, then, take your time and follow the instructions of God without minding how anyone around you will feel. As long as you are in the good book of God, you are

Why Many People Are Not Successful In Life

securely secured. If God is with you, there is no human being, or any agent of the devil that can stand successfully against you.

Beloved, if you don't want to fail in life then, my advice to you this day is that you should always follow Gods instruction no matter whose ego is affected. It is always better and also to your advantage if you offend man and be in the good book of God. The reason is that man may give you recognition, but if God does not give you recognition your life is at a great risk. Don't sell your future for a token. Your future is meant to be glorious don't throw it into the dustbin with your hands.

You Are Born To Be Great

4. PRIDE

Pride is another reason why people fail to succeed in life. This may sound funny and meaningless to you but it is real thing. Pride is a subtle killer. It kills its victims in a way that they will not know that it is pride that is killing them. It usually operates under a cover of self deception.

The bible says:

> *Pride goeth before destruction, and an haughty spirit before a fall.*
> *Prov. 16:18*

What is pride? Pride is you seeing yourself above how God is seeing you. Pride is you calling yourself what you are not. It is giving yourself a false image before men.

Why Many People Are Not Successful In Life

For instance, you cannot afford to conveniently pay for a three bedroom apartment, yet you go ahead and rent a four bedroom duplex. You may think you are impressing some people but the truth is that you are actually mortgaging your future. Always try and live your size at every point of your life.

One of my senior pastors shared a story about his life with me some years back, and it perfectly explains what we are talking about here. He said one day God told him to close his ministry and go work in another pastor's ministry, but he refused to obey God's instruction because he already have a 'struggling' ministry.

Some months later, the Pastor that the Lord asked him to go and work with called a

You Are Born To Be Great

national meeting of all his branch pastors and gave out all the branches to whoever is the pastor in charge. Then the Lord told him that He wanted to help that my senior pastor, but pride has deprived him of that Divine help. What a great pity. What a useless way to loose divine plan. What a cheap way to miss divine provision.

Pride is one of the instruments the devil has used over the ages past as well as in the present era to destroy the glorious destiny of many people; and this is possible because they are gullible to his evil devices.

One other very important thing you must know about pride is that once it possesses you, it will turn you into the enemy of God, and you know just as I do that it is always very dangerous for any one to become the

Why Many People Are Not Successful In Life

enemy of God. You must kill pride if you don't want pride to kill your glorious destiny.

The bible says:

> *But he giveth more grace. Wherefore he saith, God resisteth the proud but giveth grace unto the humble.*
> ***James 4:6***

The word of God also says:

> *The LORD will destroy the house of the proud: but he will establish the border of the widow.*
> ***Proverbs 15:25***

Friend, it will be in your own interest to see that you destroy the spirit of pride out of your life before the spirit of pride destroys your glorious future. Be humble before God

You Are Born To Be Great

and with men because that is the secret of Divine promotion. Pride has been the reason for the fall of many people, never allow yourself to become one of them. The more humble you become, the more the grace that will attend to you.

5. LACK OF FOCUS

Many people also fail in life because they suddenly lost focus of who they are or where they are going in life. I want you to know that there are many things that will be contending for your attention on your way to greatness, but if you give any of such side attractions any attention, it will surely distract you from getting to your desired destination.

To get yourself involved with too many

Why Many People Are Not Successful In Life

things at the same time under the excuse of multiple source of income is dangerous to your success. When you become a man of crowded vision you will surely derail. Please watch it. One thing you must know is that there are many things you will never be able to do successfully because you are not cut out for them.

Distraction therefore, are the things that are constantly seeking your attention in order to distract you from reaching your destination. You must know what you need in life and face it. This is very important. Otherwise, you will see yourself where you never plan to be. Always learn to face where you are going with every energy in you. You may invest your money in some other ventures as you are led by the Holy Spirit,

You Are Born To Be Great

but try and be known for something in particular. If you try to be a jack of all trade, you will end up as a master of none.

Have you ever seen a man pursuing two rats at the same time? What do you think he will get at the end of the day? He will catch nothing. This is the same way it has been with people who give room to distraction in the journey of life. At the end of the day, they will have nothing to show for their efforts.

6. MIS-USE OF OPPORTUNITIES

One other reason why many people end their lives as a failure is that they mis-use the opportunities that comes their way in the journey of life. You see, God keep giving us opportunities but most people have

Why Many People Are Not Successful In Life

constantly abuse them and at the end of the day, they will have to contend with many problems and obstacles.

For instance, a man suddenly finds himself in the possession of say one million naira, and the first thing he could think of doing is to change his wardrobe and get a new car, without thinking on any investment. By the time he will know what is happening he has finished spending the whole money. And he will now start to look for money to do business. That is the problem with many people in our society.

The trinkets and necklaces inside some peoples wardrobe are more than the money they need to start a business. This is foolishness in the highest form. Please, learn how to make the best of the chances

You Are Born To Be Great

or opportunities God brings your way all the time and you will see that the journey of life has been designed to favour you by God.

The above mentioned points are just few among the many reasons why people fail in life. But one thing I do know is that if you can take care of the above mentioned points, they will go a long way to put you in a position of command so that you will be able to take good care of the others around you.

Failure is a choice and success is also a choice. The one you chose is the one you will surely get. But I advice you to choose success by going determinedly in pursuit of the points shared above. That is the best choice you must made without any second thought.

Why Many People Are Not Successful In Life

You can get a copy of my book: **YOU HAVE NO EXCUSE TO FAIL** for more information about this subject. It is a book that will surely help you to achieve more than you think you can.

You Are Born To Be Great

3 STEPS TO GREATNESS

It is a common knowledge among men that every success has a secret. A wise man has said that if you really want to know the secret of any successful man, all you need to do is to go and read his story. Because you will always find the secret of every successful man inside his stories.

Every child of God that is thirsty for genuine greatness must be ready to obey the instructions of the only great and very successful God. Greatness does not just fall

You Are Born To Be Great

on anyone's laps. You must walk your way up into greatness if you truly desire to be great. You must be ready to pay the price of greatness if you want to enjoy the dividend of greatness in your endeavours. Learning from the people who have done successfully what you are doing now is one of the easiest way to become a record breaker in life.

The followings are among the secret to greatness as revealed by the wisdom of God. Please, take your time to digest them very well, and I can assure you that your world will soon hear about you. I want you to know that the word of God can never fail. When you act according to the instructions of His word, you will get good result - GREAT SUCCESS.

Steps To Greatness

1. YOU MUST BE BORN AGAIN.

One thing that you must know is that a canal man can not fulfil the demands of the Spirit of God. To enjoy Spiritual gifts, you must be spiritual. For you to enjoy divine revelations, you must be born again.

> *Jesus answered and said unto him, verily, verily, I say unto thee, Expect a man be born again, he cannot see the kingdom of God.*
>
> *Nicodemus saith unto him, how can a man be born again when he his old? Can he entered the second time into his mother's womb and be born?.*
>
> *Jesus answered verily, verily, I say unto thee, except a man be born of water and of spirit, he cannot enter into the kingdom*

You Are Born To Be Great

of God.
John 3:3-5

Hear this; you can never know a fearful man, until there is an occasion for him to fear. Also, you can never know who is a thief until there is an opportunity for him to steal. In the same way, you can never know who is a genuine child of God until your faith or believe in the word of God is tested.

When Adam fell in the Garden of Eden, the spirit of God in him died. Man became separated from God. Jesus came and restored the life of God back into man, but this is infused into man only at salvation. You must experience a genuine new birth before you can have access into the things of God. You can only be connected to God through His Spirit.

Steps To Greatness

In the gospel according to Saint John, the word of God says:

> *But as many as received him, to them gave he power to become the children of God, even to them that believe on his name.*
> *John 1:12*

The truth is that it is only when you are connected to the spirit of God that you can receive instructions from Him. He that is of the flesh cannot please God. It is the spirit that quickens, the flesh profits nothing.

The first key to greatness is that you must be born again. It is not optional, it is the REAL thing, and it is very important. It is the starting point to your world of great exploits.

You Are Born To Be Great

ARE YOU TRULY BORN AGAIN?

In the body of Christ today, there are many people who claimed that they are born again, but when you have the opportunity to examine their ways of living, you will see that they are not what they claimed to be.

Consider this: if your life is not governed by the word of God you are not truly born again. Even if you choose to turn the church into your bedroom, and make the holy Bible your head rest, if the word of God is not the director and commander of your life affairs, then, the truth is that you are not born again. There is no amount of explanation that can justify your disobedience to His word.

According to the book of 1 Peter, the word of God says;

Steps To Greatness

Being born again not of corruptible seed but of the incorruptible by the word of God which lives and abide for ever.
1 Peter 1:23

If you are the child of God who still make choices with the word of God according to your feelings and emotions, then you are not born again.

TAKE NOTE OF THIS

If the word of God cannot compel you to do certain things and refrain you from doing certain things, then your claim of being born again is a fake.

Sometimes ago, I had a very bad experience with a man of God. My wife was sick and I was led by the Holy Spirit to talk to him for assistance. So I went to his house. I discussed the matter of my wife's health problem with him and he followed me down to our house. He prayed with us, and when he was going he gave to us the exact amount the Holy Spirit has told me to ask from him. When this man of God returned to his house, another brother went to see him for a reason I cannot tell, but this man of God began to say some bad words to this brother about me.

When this brother left the pastor's house, he came to my place and told me everything that pastor said. So I became angry with the pastor and dressed up to go to his house. I was determined to go and fight him, but as I stepped out of my house the Holy Spirit instructed me to get back.

I became troubled and upset because the Lord had refrained me from carrying out

Steps To Greatness

my intention. What happened next was that I could not pray because my spirit was chocked by the event. On the third day, I cautioned myself to let go because the devil may capitalize on my present situation. I began to pray in the spirit until suddenly the love of that pastor crept back into my mind. And today we are in good relationship with one another.

The point I am trying to make here is that you must be ready to obey the word of God no matter the situation. Anything that is contrary to this is from the devil.

2. DISCOVER THE PLAN OF GOD FOR YOUR LIFE

Please, understand that before God created you, He has already determined everything about your life. He actually made you for a

You Are Born To Be Great

very specific purpose.

> *Then the word of the lord came unto me saying*
>
> *Before I formed thee in the belly I knew thee: and before thou comet forth out of the womb I sanctify thee, and I ordained thee a Prophet unto the nations.*
>
> *Jeremiah 1:4-5*

This is God's word unto Jeremiah. It is also a pointer to what God has in mind concerning you. God has a very unique plan for everyone of us. It is such a unique plan that each and every one of us is in a different plan agenda of God. The plan of God for you is not what you can invent by yourself. It is there already, you only have to discover it.

Steps To Greatness

According to the book of Jeremiah chapter one verses four and five, we can see very clearly that there are certain things that are very unique to every man and woman in the kingdom of God. This includes.

[A.] Ever before your mother conceived you, God has determined everything about you in minute detail. For instance, He knows you will be at the place where you are right now. And he knows where you are going to from where you are presently. God's knowledge about each one of us is as that detailed.

He alone knows what will happen to you before the end of today. He knows also what will happen to you tomorrow. The truth is this: everything that will happen to you, both good and bad, depending on how you live your life, from the very beginning to the end of your life is known to him in details.

You Are Born To Be Great

You cannot hide from Him. The earlier you fall in line with His will for your life the better it is for you.

[B.] While you are still in your mother's womb, God has determined and concluded what you must become in life. Your assignment has been determined and gloriously concluded. Some folks have read what they studied in the school just to fulfil all righteousness because, what they have studied is their making, or that of their parent or the result of the frustrations they have encountered. They didn't hear it from God as His will for them.

Many of the medical doctors we have around are not destined to prosper as a doctor but as a politician. Some people must become traders, and others school teachers and lecturers. Some people must

Steps To Greatness

become hair dressers and barbers according to the original plan of God for their lives. Many graduates of law now will end up as bankers if they must prosper according to the agenda of God. Some as financial experts in order to become giants in life.

The truth is this: trying to create a life or a future for yourself that is different from the original plan of God for you is nothing but a wasted exercise. It will never work. You cannot become the great man or woman God has made you through your own will but by following His will.

If God has designed you to be a lawyer, and you are trying to become a medical doctor you may graduate as a medical doctor but you cannot achieve the height he has planned for you through medical practice.

You Are Born To Be Great

Please, take note of this point very well, because you don't have two lives to live.

CONSIDER THIS TESTIMONY

There was a lady who returned back to Nigeria from the United Kingdom after she was trained as a nurse over there in the UK. According to her story, she had worked for so many years without anything to show for her struggles.

On getting back to Nigeria, someone took her to a man of God for prayers. And while praying the Holy Spirit revealed to the man of God that according to the plan of God for that lady she is expected to be a trader, trading in palm oil and not working as a nurse. Isn't that amazing as well as wonderful?

At first she resisted that revelation from the

Steps To Greatness

Holy Spirit, but, after many years of more struggling, she decided to do what God has ordained for her life. The most striking thing is that within very few months of walking in the will of God for her life, her story changed and she was living well. What she could not achieve through the nursing profession, she achieved by doing what God has designed for her without stress.

Friend, it is better for you to locate what God has made you, otherwise, you may struggle through life and end up as a failure. You will not miss the plan of God for your life in Jesus name.

Let me tell you this also: many are in the will of God for their life but they see themselves as incapable to become what God has made them. Inferiority complex is the reason for the calamities this set of

You Are Born To Be Great

people are going through now. Trying to be someone else is the reason for the failure of many. The fact that your friend is a successful preacher does not mean you will become successful through preaching except it is from the Lord.

HOW DO I KNOW I AM IN THE WILL OF GOD?

Many people are engaged in certain vocations not because they like it, but because that is what they or someone else wants them to do. Some are forcing themselves to please other people's desire simply because they don't want to offend anybody, but they have failed to realize the fact that their life is at a risk.

The best way to know if you are doing the

Steps To Greatness

will of God or not is for you to sit down and ask yourself some fundamental questions, like:

1. Who told me to do what I am doing?- Myself, my parent, my friend, or God?

Your ability to answer this question sincerely and without any external influence will go a long way to help you to become what God has destined you to become.

2. Why am I doing what I am doing presently?- To fulfill God's purpose for my life or to please someone else?

3. Do I like what I am doing now or not? Or am I forcing myself to like it?

If you can answer the above questions very

You Are Born To Be Great

sincerely without any deception, you will be amazed to discover that you are not only unique, you are made to become a champion in your generation.

3. LIVE A RIGHTEOUS LIFE

Righteousness must become your way of life. You cannot afford sin to deprive you of the glorious future God has planned for you. If you do, it simply shows that you are not wise.

It is only righteousness that promotes a man. Sin always bring shame, disgrace and failure. Your choice therefore must be the eradication of sin by all means from your life. There must be no second thought about this. Your firm decision must be to live above sin so that you may constantly please your God.

Steps To Greatness

Hear this: whatever is the price for you to pay in other for you to become righteous, please pay. It is better for you to pay the price of being righteous than for you to suffer the reproach of sin in the future.

According to the book of Proverbs the word of God says:

> *But the path of the just is like a shining light, that shineth more and more unto the perfect day.*
> *Proverbs 4:18*

Also, in the book of Isaiah, the word of God says:

> *The way of the just is upright: thou, most upright, dost weigh the path of the just.*
> *Isaiah 26:7*

You Are Born To Be Great

The word of God also says in the book of James the following mind-blowing words. It says:

> *Confess your faults one to another, and pray one for another that ye may be healed. The effectual fervent prayer of a righteous man availeth much.*
>
> *James 5:16*

Friend, without your readiness to live above sin, your walk with God will yield no good result at the end because, God can never bless the sinner. In fact, if you care to know, the truth is that every sinner is an enemy of God.

4. BE DETERMINED TO SUCCEED

Success or failure are products of your personal decision. If you decide to fail you

Steps To Greatness

will, and if you decide to succeed you will succeed. It is all about the decision you make, either consciously or otherwise.

Success and wishes are not birds of the same feather. The two will never flock together no matter how hard you try. If therefore, you are wishing to succeed but fail to do the things that bring success, you will surely fail.

Another truth you may not like to hear is that you can never become what you have not decided to become. What you cannot see you cannot become. This is very important.

Your decision to succeed therefore will always produce a definite line of action on your part when it is genuine. Every genuine decision always places a great

You Are Born To Be Great

responsibility upon you. If your decision is not driving you towards becoming responsible for certain things then it is all a fake decision.

> *But Daniel purpose in his heart that he would not defile himself with the portion of the King's meat, nor with the wine which he drank: therefore he requested of the prince of the eunuchs that he might not defile himself.*
> *Daniel 1:8*

Daniel decided not to fail even as a captive, he subsequently took steps to see that no side attraction will be able to subvert or distract his decision to succeed. He moved quickly and told the man in charge of their welfare to take away from him all the king's food and drinks so that the smell will not cause a problem to him through his nose.

Steps To Greatness

Many people have surrendered themselves to side attractions, and that is why they cannot get far with their decisions. When you have decided to win, you will know by yourself because, your actions will work in the direction of the actualisation of your decisions.

WHAT ARE SIDE ATTRACTIONS

Side attractions are the things seeking to catch your attention, in order to distract your focus, thereby disturbing you from reaching your destination. The truth is that success and luck have nothing in common. They are like two parallel lines. And it does not matter what you do, or how intelligent you are, you cannot make two parallel lines to meet.

If therefore you are waiting for luck in your

quest for greatness, then, you must realize that you may have to wait for eternity to come in other for you to get your desires met.

5. LEARN HOW TO TURN YOUR TRIALS INTO TESTIMONIES

For every problem there is a cause. You can never see a smoke anywhere without a fire burning somewhere. This is a truth you cannot change, no matter how hard you try.

You can only successfully solve a problem when you know the cause of that problem. If you don't know the cause of your problem, you cannot solve that problem. The best you can do with such problem is to guess or go through trial by error.

The prodigal son regained his life from total

destruction simply by going back to the root of his problem. Instead of guessing as to what he should do, he simply went back to beg his father for mercy. [Luke 15:17-24]

The truth is that what no one knows about your problem you will know. There is no reason why you should be deceiving yourself saying that you don't know what is happening to you. Be sincerely sincere to yourself at least to save your life from total degradation. Any one may not know what is the cause of your problem, but you and God knows. So, if there is no one to tell you the truth, please, speak the truth to yourself.

6. BE FINANCIALLY SMART

To succeed in life, we must be smart with the way we handle our finances. We must handle every of our expenses with every carefulness. There must be no room given to any expenses that is not needed. Every impromptu spending must be dealt with without mercy. Can I be sincere with you? Prayer and fasting, as good as they are, cannot help you to solve your financial problems if you are not disciplined in the way you handle your expenses and income.

I will not say much about this here because I have dealt with it in detail in my book: **CREATING GENERATIONAL WEALTH.** I will therefore advise you to get your copy of that book, you will be greatly blessed.

7. FOLLOW GOD'S INSTRUCTIONS

Instructions always make us a high-flier in life. When we talk about instruction, your opinion is irrelevant. You only need to carry out instructions, you don't analyze

Steps To Greatness

instructions. And you don't amend instructions. Instructions are meant to be carried out. Simple.

If therefore you are interested to succeed in life, it will do you a great good if you learn how to follow the instructions of God for you at any point and no matter how you feel about it. I want you to know that God knows what you don't know and He can do what you cannot do. He also knows the future from the very beginning. Every wise children of God will never argue with any Divine instruction. They are careful enough to simply flow into it because, they know that the result that will come from their act of obedience will be great. **[Ezek' 37:3-10]**

8. LIVE A PRAYERFUL LIFE

You Are Born To Be Great

There is nothing you can do successfully without being prayerful. You must be ready to pray your way through. Like they say; what is good needs prayer to remain good, and what is bad needs prayer to become good. A good prayer life must become your way of life.

Jesus Himself lived a very prayerful life and the early Apostles followed His foot-step. No wonder why they were able to make such outstanding success in their time. Nothing can be more true than this.

Friend, to be prayer-less is to become a prey in the hand of the enemy. Remember the devil is roaming about to locate that careless Christian who he may devour. You will not become a prey to the devil in Jesus name.

Steps To Greatness

The more prayerful you become the more success you will achieve because, as a prayerful man, you have become a terror to the devil and his host. Also, I want you to know that the more prayerful you become the more divine revelation you will enjoy.

Please, do your best to get my book on prayer titled: **GUIDE TO EFFECTIVE PRAYER** and learn more about how you can live a successful prayerful life as a genuine child of God. You will not fail in Jesus name.

You Are Born To Be Great

THE IN-EVITABLE

Having come this far, I need to remind you again that failure is a choice and success is also a choice. And the beauty of it is that you will always get the one you choose to have at any particular point in time.

For instance, if you gather together twenty boys this year, in the next ten years you will be amazed to realize that they will not be at the same level in terms of achievement. The question is why?

You Are Born To Be Great

The truth is that each one of them will be at different levels according to their individual's input into the issues of their life. Individual's responsiveness to the responsibilities of their life as they move forward in life will determine the level of achievement each one will record at the end of the tenth year.

Your input will determine your level of achievement per time. This is the blunt truth you cannot resist. If you can pay adequate attention to the issues of your life and refuse to leave them to chances, then you will determine the space of the great things that will be happening in your life.

The In-evitable

DIFFERENCES BETWEEN A FAILURE AND A SUCCESSFUL PERSON?

1. Failures are **SUCCESSFUL** people who give up too soon. Isn't that amazing? There are many folks who will quit whatever they are into because of a little challenge that comes across their way. This is not only bad, it is always the best and the fastest way to the "island" of the great failures.

2. Successful people on the other hand are the **FAILURES** who refuse to give up. Whatever happens, they are ready to see the end of the journey they have started. Every challenge will make them stronger to take the next step.

Friend, anyone will become a failure if he or she does not know how to hold on. Quitters have never win once, and successful people

You Are Born To Be Great

have never quite at all in whatever they do.

The main point that distinguished failures from the successful individuals is their **actions** and **dispositions** to the events that happens to them in the course of their endeavours.

You will not fail again in Jesus name.

I decree in the name of Jesus that the last failure you recorded is the last one for ever in Jesus name.

Thank you and God bless you.

Welcome on board the flight of the champions.

VERY PRECIOUS INFORMATION

Friend, have you ever considered giving your life to the Lord Jesus as something of a very great importance, and which you must do with much urgency? If you have not done it before, I strongly advise that you do it **TODAY,** because another day may be too late.

Please, understand this: without Jesus Christ as the Lord over your life, your life is not only useless, it is also at a great risk. Any life without Christ is also faced with many crises.

Jesus Christ is calling you today, please don't refuse His call of love, neither harden your heart to His outstretched arm of grace towards you.

God will bless you richly as you yield to His glorious call to you today in Jesus name.

You are welcome into His glorious and life-changing kingdom.

For More Spiritual Help Write To:
P.O. Box 7035, Sapon Abeokuta
Ogun State, Nigeria.

E-mail: twph2013@gmail.com
Phone: 0813 666 2194, 0802 706 5871

What This Ministry Is All About

The activities of Samuel Olulana Ministries includes:

1. **Radio-** The radio broadcast, "Wisdom Impact", is reaching thousand of lives across the nations of the world.

2. **Television-** Overcomers hour, an internationally syndicated weekly programme features teachings on God's principles for living an overcomer's life.

3. **WLBI-** The ministerial training arm through which those who are in the ministry, and those preparing for ministry is trained for effective ministry work.

4. **Missions-** The ministry involved in serious mission project across the nations of the world.

5. **Literature-** Best-selling books and magazines through which the wisdom of and power of God are proclaimed.

6. **Crusades/Seminars-** Multitudes are ministered to at crusades and seminars across the globe, as Samuel Olulana declares the life-changing principles of God.

Other Books
By
Samuel O. Olulana

1. Creating Generational Wealth
2. Living In Dominion
3. Maximizing The Power Of Purpose
4. Turning Your Problem Into Testimonies
5. Understanding The Secret Of Victorious Living
6. Benefits Of Walking In Obedience
7. The Forsaken Truth
8. You shall Not Be Barren
9. Walking In The Miraculous
10. Enjoying Financial Dominion
11. Benefits Of Living Your Life On Purpose
12. Guide To Effective Prayer
13. You Have No Excuse To Fail
14. overcoming the challenges Of Life
15. How To Overcome Your Struggles
16. Wisdom For Uncommon Success
17. Enjoying The Unlimited Power Of The Unlimited
18. Wisdom For Daily Living

Get Your Copies Of:
Rev. OLULANA SAMUEL
LIFE-TRANSFORMING BOOKS & CD'S

These books and Cd's will open your mind to

KEYS TO GREATNESS IN LIFE

Available in many Christian bookshops across the nation

<u>Or Call:</u> 0813 666 2194;
0802 706 5876

You will be glad you did.

SEND YOUR PRAYER REQUESTS THROUGH THIS PAGE:
Please pray along with me on the following issues:

Please send this subscription / prayer sheet to:

SAMUEL OLULANA MINISTRIES INTERNATIONAL
P. O. BOX 7035, SAPON, ABEOKUTA, OGUN STATE, NIGERIA.

www.ingramcontent.com/pod-product-compliance
Lightning Source LLC
Chambersburg PA
CBHW031404040426
42444CB00005B/411